LIFE STORY

SHARK

MICHAEL CHINERY

Photography by

David Doubilet, Jack Jackson

Pat Morris, Allan Power, Ken Lucas

Illustrated by

Martin Camm

Troll Associates

Library of Congress Cataloging-in-Publication Data

Chinery, Michael.
    Shark / by Michael Chinery; illustrated by Martin Camm;
photographs by David Doubilet...[et al.].
        p.   cm.—(Life story)
    Summary: Describes the physical characteristics, behavior, and
varieties of sharks.
    ISBN 0-8167-2104-1 (lib. bdg.)   ISBN 0-8167-2105-X (pbk.)
    1. Sharks—Juvenile literature. [1. Sharks.] I. Camm, Martin,
ill. II. Doubilet, David, ill. III. Title. IV. Series.
QL638.9.C46 1991
597´.31—dc20   90-33361

Published by Troll Associates

This edition published in 2003.

Designed by James Marks

Printed in the U.S.A.

10 9 8 7 6 5

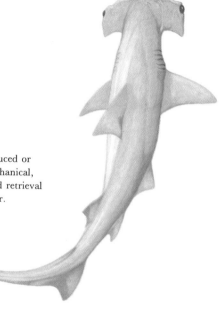

INTRODUCTION

This book is about some of the fiercest animals in the sea – the fast-moving sharks. You can learn how these fish smell their prey from a distance and then cut it to pieces with their razor-sharp teeth. You can discover that some sharks give birth to babies, while others lay eggs in tough cases, and you will find out that sharks do not make good parents. Meet the world's largest fish – the Whale shark – and discover what *it* feeds on.

Sharks are some of the most frightening animals in the sea. Look at this Great White shark and you'll see why. The teeth of this monster are up to two and a half inches (6 cm) long and their razor-sharp edges can slice right through a man's leg. Sharks have several rows of teeth, and when one row wears out another row moves forward to take its place.

Different kinds of sharks have different kinds of teeth. A shark can even cause a nasty wound just by bumping into someone, because its skin is covered with small toothlike scales and is very rough. Divers photographing sharks often work in steel cages like the one you see in the picture.

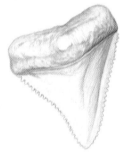

Most sharks are designed for speed.
A flick of the tail sends the graceful,
streamlined body through the water at
speeds of up to 43 miles per hour (69 kph).
Sharks' fins are not like those of other
fish. Instead of having delicate, fanlike
fins, sharks have thick flaps of skin.

The broad front fins, which you can
see very clearly in the photograph, are
like wings, and they help the shark keep
its balance as it swims through the
water. The first sign of an approaching
shark is usually the big triangular fin on
the back. It often sticks right out of the
water.

Like all fish, sharks breathe with gills.
These are rows of tiny blood-filled
"fingers" on each side of the shark's
head. Water flowing over the gills gives
up its oxygen to the shark's
bloodstream. The water comes in
through the mouth while the shark
swims.

After passing over the gills, the water
leaves the body through slits behind the
head. There are usually five of these gill
slits on each side, but the Seven Gilled
shark in the photograph has seven slits
on each side.

A shark's nostrils, shown in the
drawing, are used only for smelling and
have nothing to do with breathing.

Sharks feed mainly on other fish. Some of the larger ones eat seals, and some will attack people if they get the chance.

Sharks find their food mainly by smell, and groups of them may gather around one large victim. The sharks in the photograph are getting very excited because they can smell the blood of a dead fish. When this happens, they sometimes go into a feeding frenzy and attack anything in sight – even lumps of wood floating in the water.

The Thresher sharks in the drawing are using their long tails to herd small fish into a group before eating them.

Most fish have an air-filled bag in their bodies. It is called a swim bladder, and it helps them to float in the water. Sharks don't have swim bladders, and they sink to the bottom if they stop swimming.

The Cat shark in the drawing is resting on the sea bed, although it is not really asleep. Some sharks, like the Gray Reef shark, seek out caves and other special areas where they can rest. There are sometimes so many sharks in these places that they pile on top of each other.

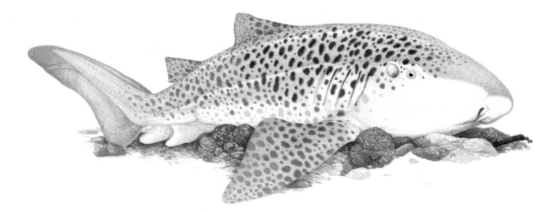

Not all sharks are sleek and graceful swimmers. The strange-looking creature in the photograph looks more like a lump of rock than a shark. It is a Carpet shark. It is not built for speed like most of the other sharks, because it doesn't have to chase other animals for food. It spends most of its time on the sea bed and snaps up any fish or other creature that comes along.

The colorful False Cat shark has a low first dorsal fin. The Angel shark gets its name from its big, winglike fins. The Hammerhead shark is another weird-looking shark, with its eyes at the sides of its hammer-shaped head. It is a fast-swimming and very dangerous shark.

The Whale shark is the biggest fish in the world. It can grow to more than 40 feet (12 m) in length and can weigh over 15 tons (13.5 metric tons). It dwarfs the diver in the photograph, but he is in no danger. The Whale shark is a peaceful animal that feeds mainly on small, shrimplike creatures. It gulps water into its huge mouth and strains all the animals from it before squirting the water out again through its gill slits.

16

The Basking shark, shown in the drawing, feeds in the same way. Look at its enormous gill slits. These are necessary because of the huge amounts of water that pass through the fish while it is feeding.

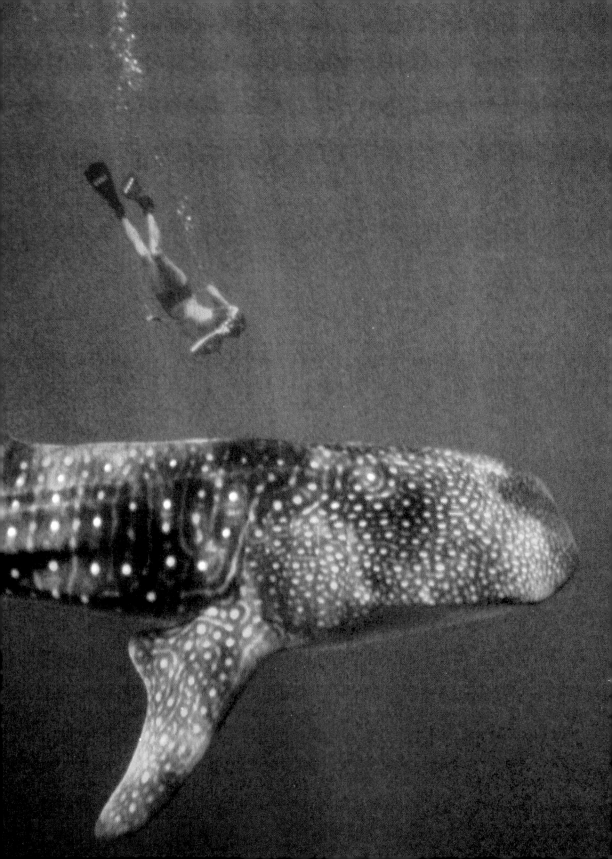

There are about 350 different kinds of sharks in the oceans, but they are not all big. Some sharks, such as the Cigar shark (top drawing), are less than eight inches (20 cm) long and can fit on a man's hand.

Dogfish (bottom drawing) are small sharks that usually live around the coast.

The fish in the photograph is a Horn shark. It has poisonous spines on its back. It can grow to nearly six feet (2 m) in length, but it is a slow mover and feeds mainly on shellfish on the sea bed.

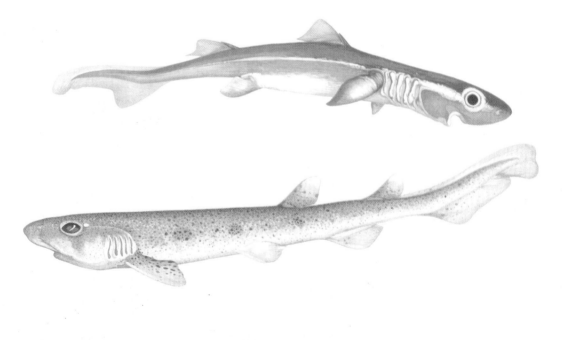

The shark in the photograph is a female Gray Reef shark. A male is chasing the female and dancing around her. He may even bite her, but these fish are not really fighting. They are courting and will eventually mate. Most large sharks probably mate while swimming.

The male often clings to the female with his teeth, but the bite marks he leaves on her fins and body soon heal. After mating, the female will either lay eggs or give birth to live young.

Sharks that lay eggs always lay them in tough, horny cases. These cases are often called mermaids' purses. The one in the photograph was laid by a Swell shark, and it is firmly fixed to some coral, so it does not float away.

A baby fish is growing inside the case, as you can see in the drawing. It feeds on the yolk that is in its egg. The baby grows slowly, and it may be a year old before it is ready to chew its way out of the case and swim away.

The Whale shark lays the world's biggest egg. It measures about 12 inches (30.5 cm) long, 5½ inches (14 cm) wide and is about 4 inches (10 cm) thick.

The baby Lemon shark in the big picture has just been born. You can clearly see the cord which attached this shark to the inside of its mother's body, but not all baby sharks are attached to their mothers in this way. The cord will break as the young fish swims off. The baby can take care of itself right away.

Like many other sharks, the Lemon shark usually has four babies at a time. Some sharks have only two babies. Others have as many as 60 babies. It can take up to two years for the shark babies to grow inside their mothers.

Shark babies can swim and hunt for food as soon as they are born. Their mothers don't usually take care of them at all. In fact, adult sharks will eat their babies if they get the chance.

The baby Whitetip shark in the photograph is hiding in a coral reef where the adults can't reach it. The young shark will dart out to catch other fish, and then hide again. Even when it is fully grown it won't be completely safe, because sharks often eat each other. In fact, a shark's worst natural enemy is another shark.

The striped fish swimming with the young shark in the photograph is called a remora or a suckerfish. It uses a large sucker on top of its head to cling to the shark's body, but it doesn't do the shark any harm. It is a lazy fish and it just uses the shark as a taxi.

The remora catches other small fish, and also eats scraps dropped by the shark. Most sharks have remoras for company, as well as pilot fish, like those in the drawing. People used to think that pilot fish guided sharks through the water, but this is not true. The pilot fish just swim around the sharks and wait for scraps of food.

Fascinating facts

The skin of the Whale shark is thicker than that of any other animal. It is often as much as eight inches (20 cm) thick.

Sharks have skeletons, but they are not made of real bone. They are made of a softer material called cartilage. This is the same elastic material that makes up the tip of your nose.

Sailors and fishermen used to use the rough skins of dogfish and other sharks to scrub the wooden decks of their ships. Some of these skins were also dried and used as sandpaper for smoothing woodwork.

Some sharks can smell blood in the water from more than a mile away.

They can hear things even farther away, but their relatively small eyes can't see things more than about 65 feet (20 m) away.

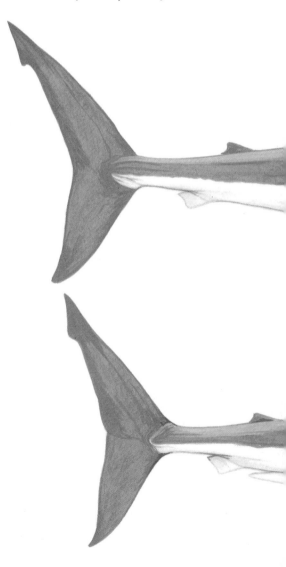

Female sharks are often much larger than males of the same kind.

Baby sharks are often called pups.

A hungry shark will eat almost anything it can find. One shark caught in the sea near Italy had three overcoats and a raincoat in its stomach!

Great White sharks – female (*above*) and male (*below*).

Index

Angel shark 14

baby sharks 22, 24, 26, 31
Basking shark 16
blood 10, 30
bloodstream 8
breathing 8

Carpet shark 14
cartilage 30
Cat shark 12
Cigar shark 18
coral 22, 26
courting 20

divers 4, 16
dogfish 18, 30

eggs 3, 20, 22
eyes 14, 30

False Cat shark 14
feeding frenzy 10
fins 6, 14, 20

gills 8
gill slits 8, 16
Gray Reef shark 12, 20
Great White shark 4, 30-31

Hammerhead shark 14
hearing 30
Horn shark 18

Lemon shark 24

mating 20
mermaids' purse 22
mouth 8, 16

nostrils 8

oxygen 8

pilot fish 28

remora 28

scales 4
seals 10
shellfish 18
skeleton 30
skin 4, 30
smell 3, 8, 10, 30
speed 6, 14, 18
spines 18
suckerfish 28
Swell shark 22
swim bladder 12

tail 6, 10
teeth 3, 4, 20
Thresher shark 10

Whale shark 3, 16, 22, 30
Whitetip shark 26